Twelve
Town Trails
in Cheshire

To Joan
Best wishes,
Jen Darling

Jen Darling

ALFRESCO
publications

First published in 1991 by Alfresco Publications

7 Pineways, Appleton, Warrington, Cheshire WA4 5EJ

Cover Design by Paul Marsh

Cover Photograph by John Cocks,
with permission from Cheshire Life

Typeset by Jen Darling

Designed & Printed by CPS Press

Maps drawn by Mike Evans

PREFACE

Town Trails is the first in a new series of books reflecting various aspects of the county of Cheshire: 'Village Strolls', then three books of family cycle rides by Lyn Goodkin are to follow. This book has twelve trails, each one giving a different insight into the make-up of the area. The distance walked varies between one and six miles and a sketchmap is provided with each. The routes are also enlivened by snippets of local and natural history.

It is hoped that families will enjoy these trails and a park or open space is mentioned wherever possible as a suitable venue for a picnic and where children can 'let off steam'. Hopefully, each Trail may also provide a painless way of giving youngsters an early glimpse into history which may be fostered in later life.

Several of the shorter trails are also aimed at those of more mature years who, although their stile-climbing days are over, still enjoy a gentle stroll. These walks provide them with, not only a breath of fresh air and some exercise, but also with some interesting sights to pick out along the way. They would also be negotiable for famiies encumbered by a pram, pushchair, or even a wheelchair in the case of Sandbach and Whitchurch.

All these trails were written originally as articles for *Cheshire Life*, appearing in the magazine during 1990 and 1991, and I am delighted to have been given permission to republish them in book form. I would also like to thank Jane Fickling, the magazine's former editor, who had the original idea for the series, and Patrick O'Neill, the present editor, both for his enthusiastic support and for contributing the Foreword.

A word of thanks also to Mike Evans, who copied all the maps so meticulously, sometimes enhancing them with tiny line drawings of his own. The map of Cheshire at the front of the book shows each town's position on the County's main road network. Detailed travelling instructions are not given as any motoring atlas will provide these from any direction. However, directions to the free parking at the starting point of every Trail are included in the text.

I am particularly grateful to John Cocks for contributing all the photographs, to Paul Marsh of CPS Press for the book's design, and to Valerie West for proof reading the copy and for her general support as friend and advocate! And finally, a word of appreciation for the advice and assistance provided by my dubious but long-suffering husband. (Without doubt, his wife's latest venture will provide him with a few more grey hairs and wrinkles!)

Jen Darling • *October 1991*

CONTENTS

FOREWORD

During her four years of walking the highways and byways of the county for **Cheshire Life** Jen Darling has developed a reputation which would amply justify the epithet 'the thinking woman's Wainwright'!

She is more than just a hiker of set trails or remorseless route marcher over county contours. Instead she takes a thoughtful stroll through the histories and mysteries of the towns she visits, pausing awhile to note this curious building or to recall that little bit of folklore, local custom, famous or infamous celebrity. She can read a landscape or townscape like other people read a book.

Her walks are accessible to any reader with a stout heart and strong pair of shoes, with clear instructions on where to go, where to pause - and often with a little advice on the hostelries, churches and watering points *en route*. Ranging from one to six miles the walks can also be said to represent a microcosm of Cheshire town-life.

Just as importantly they are perfectly adapted for the armchair walker, who in imagination can follow in Jen's footsteps, up hill and down vale, without ever moving from the warmth and security of his (or her) own fireside.

Patrick O'Neill
Editor of Cheshire Life

MAP OF CHESHIRE

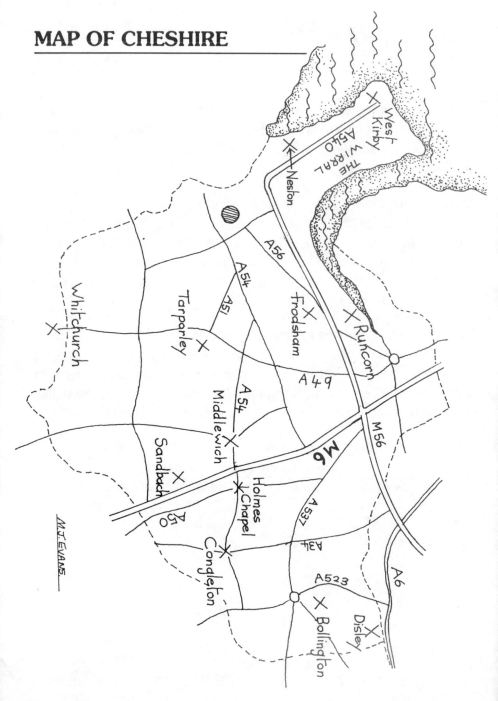

M.J. EVANS

INTRODUCTION

It is hoped that this book of twelve Town Trails will provide a small insight into Cheshire's past and present; for each town has grown for different reasons and each offers a glimpse of the county and reflects the diverse development of the area as a whole. As an appetizer to the Trails read on . . .

History
Cheshire's history goes back to prehistoric times, as these discoveries show: a dinosaur's footprint near Tarporley in the heart of the Cheshire plain, a long barrow at the Bridestones near Congleton, then traces from the Iron Age at Woodhouse hill fort above Frodsham. Later evidence of Roman occupation is to be found at Mediolanum (Whitchurch) - southern gateway to the county, and Roman roads, which include King Street, circle Condate (Middlewich). On the Wirral coast, Norsemen from Ireland and Man settled at West Kirby where a Viking tombstone is still preserved, and evidence of a Saxon settlement has been found on Neston's site. Yet undoubtedly Cheshire's most notable treasures from that time are the Saxon crosses at Sandbach.

From later times, remnants of Civil War skirmishes are to be found throughout the region - church walls pockmarked by cannon at Holmes Chapel and Middlewich, artefacts in Tarporley church, and Sandbach's market place - still known as Scots Common from a rout that took place there.

Buildings
On many of the Trails the churches provide a well-preserved glimpse of the past. The Norman nave of Frodsham church has recently

provided an authentic film set for Robin Hood, Prince of Thieves, a swashbuckling tale if ever there was one! Unusual is the public thoroughfare through the church tower at Sandbach, a squat hearse house at Runcorn, and an epitaph in the churchyard at Middlewich which may cause many a chuckle!

The Trails also make it easy to follow the development of dwelling houses through the ages. Numerous are the 'magpie' cottages of the 17th century, especially in Sandbach, some still retaining the original wattle and daub walls and thatched roofs. Local stone was used to build the terraced cottages at Bollington, and Elizabethan architecture is displayed in the tiny manor house at Tarporley. There are Georgian terraces at Tarporley, Edwardian and Victorian villas at Middlewich, and every town boasts some architecture of note. Then there are unusual finds like the crinkle-crankle wall at Neston.

Hopefully, the architects of the 20th century will eventually show some originality and colour in their designs, leaving their stamp on the county other than in recycled mock Tudor, and drab concrete buildings like The Concourse at West Kirby and Runcorn's Shopping City.

Transport
While walking the Trails you can also follow the development of Cheshire's transport system. The short age of the stage coach is well represented, with almost every town boasting a coaching inn: the George in Sandbach, Tarporley's Swan Hotel, the Red Lion in Whitchurch, the Old Red Lion at Sandbach - to name but a few. Outside some, the stone mounting block still stands, and there is mention of cruel sports of yesteryear - as at the Bull Ring in the heart of Whitchurch, and bear baiting at Sandbach. Inside these inns today you can soak up the past while enjoying a pint of Real Ale or an appetising spread, and other pubs such as the Redway Tavern at Bollington and the Coach and Horses near Congleton also provide dishes to titillate the taste buds!

You have a glimpse back to the Canal Era while walking along Brindley's Trent & Mersey Canal at Middlewich and his Bridgewater Canal at Runcorn, while Disley boasts England's highest navigable waterway - the Peak Forest Canal. At Bollington there's Telford's picturesque Macclesfield Canal; this continues down to Congleton, where Bosley Reservoir supplies one of man's elemental needs, and a huge, high aqueduct spans the diminutive River Dane.

The 'Age of the Train' is reflected in massive, many-arched railway viaducts at Congleton and Bollington; the latter's Macclesfield to Poynton line now transformed for leisure use into the Middlewood Way. Also, far to the west The Wirral Way, running from West Kirby to Hooton, follows another dismantled line.

Bridges offer evidence of the developing road network throughout the county: the site of the Transporter Bridge at Runcorn is adjacent to the modern suspension bridge now soaring over the River Mersey and packed with traffic. We grumble, but at least it takes little time to reach the starting point of any of these Trails.

Industry
The development of industry in the region is also well represented. Salt was a commodity available at Middlewich since Roman times, and more recently Cheshire's salt deposits attracted the massive chemical industry to Runcorn - a mixed blessing perhaps!

Congleton, once well known for the manufacture of leather goods, also rivalled Macclesfield as a centre for silk weaving, and coal mining took place at Little Neston. Across the county, Bollington developed as a cotton town during the Industrial Revolution - a plethora of mill chimneys now starkly outlined against the skyline.

Towns like Tarporley, surrounded by lush agricultural land, were once markets for farm produce, with flour and cheese the main goods transported to Manchester market from there. Neston was also once an agricultural market town and a seaport for Ireland - hard to believe today with the heavily silted River Dee. Each week, the colourful stalls of street vendors can be seen during the bustling Thursday markets which have thrived since Medieval times at Sandbach, and on Frodsham's wide main street.

The author is well aware that Whitchurch is not a Cheshire town at all. Certainly, the librarian there was quick to point out that Shropshire libraries, unlike those in unenlightened Cheshire are still open all day on a Saturday - and what a blessing that proved to be! However, Whitchurch is certainly the southern gateway into Cheshire, and has many of our county's characteristics - cheese-making in particular.

Extensive house-building has increased the population of several towns to cope with the workers in new industry. Disley, a town bordering the Pennines and inextricably bound in the past with one of Cheshire's great estates - Lyme Park - nowadays is a dormitory town for commuters to Manchester and Stockport. Neston too, just creeping into the opposite corner of the county, provides homes for workers on Merseyside, and Frodsham is a pleasant residential retreat for workers in the industrial belt along the south bank of the River Mersey, with its massive oil and chemical works. Last but not least, and surrounded by an excellent communication network, Holmes Chapel is a commuter's paradise in the heart of the Cheshire plain.

Strictly speaking of course, West Kirby on The Wirral, is in Merseyside and many of its residents commute to jobs in Liverpool. However, in this book I have pandered to those Wirral folk who still consider the area to be a part of Cheshire. (Geographically of course it is, only bureaucracy has recently decreed otherwise!) Indeed, after several requests to include them in the county a later book in this series may well be 'Walks in the Wirral'.

Fact and Fancy
Each town has its war memorial, and outstanding monuments catch

the eye - the Caldy Column at West Kirby (once a warning beacon for mariners), the folly of White Nancy, high above Bollington on the Kerridge ridge. Glorious views from The Cloud above Congleton and Frodsham Hill (plus a tiny taste of the Sandstone Trail) uplift the soul, and bird life on Hilbre Island (facing West Kirby in the Dee estuary) is worth a detour. Water sports and a prestigious annual tennis tournament - precursor to Wimbledon - also offer variety in that town.

Interesting facts concerning famous people abound: John Wesley spent a night at Holmes Chapel and preached at Neston; Turner painted sunsets at West Kirby; Anthony Salvin designed All Saints' church (Runcorn); the musician, Sir Edward German, spent his childhood at Whitchurch, and Nelson landed at Neston's quay when on his clandestine visits to Lady Hamilton.

Examples of local lore and legend add colour to the scene: smugglers on the Dee's shore at Neston, the Hogg Bank boggart of Disley, and the ghostly grey lady of the Old Hall Hotel, Sandbach. Memories of local customs too are evoked: the Wakes Week at Middlewich, Race Week at Tarporley, and the Ladies' Day Parade at Neston - an annual event which still takes place.

Hopefully, the Trails described throughout these pages will provide a tantalising taste of the best that has been preserved and packed into this inimitable English county which we call Cheshire. Stretching from the Pennine hills to the Irish Sea, and described affectionately by some as a truncated teapot, its towns offer a rich variety of scene well worth discovering.

ABOVE BOLLINGTON

Distance: **3 miles**

I n the Pennine foothills at the northern end of the Saddle of Kerridge, Bollington unfolds - a higgledy-piggledy mosaic of grey, stone cottages and massive mills, their soaring chimneys separated by steep terraces, built last century to house the workforce. The intricate network of streets is sliced by both canal and defunct rail link. Each adapted to suit the leisure-time interests of today's population, Bollington is most definitely a town which moves with the times.

From the long main street (Wellington Road) turn down Adlington Road to the Middlewood Way car park. In the railway era this was a busy station, employing thirteen staff in its heyday when the gentry, together with their horse and carriage, would travel by rail to London. From 1921 to 1935 an

Bollington - a mill town nestling in the Pennine foothills   *John Cocks*

1

unusual petrol electric railcar known as the Bollington Bug also operated along this line.

Sadly, this section, stretching from Rose Hill (Marple) to Macclesfield, was closed in the Beeching cuts of 1970, only to be resurrected fifteen years later as a sandy bridleway enjoyed by ramblers, riders and cyclists, and with access for wheelchairs at several points. Here, toilets, a children's play area and the Vale Inn cater for differing needs and there is access to the massive 22-arched viaduct that spans the River Dean and gives a dizzying view over the town.

Begin by walking over it; then leave the Way at the first bridge, crossing this and continuing for a few yards to turn right along the canal's towpath. Although now a holiday route for pleasure boats, the Macclesfield Canal was completed during 1831 to transport textiles, stone, pottery and coal. Its meandering course north-south through Cheshire's Pennine foothills links the Peak Forest Canal with the Trent-Mersey in Staffordshire.

Boats are moored tranquilly at garden ends and you soon reach the Adelphi Mill, a converted cotton mill once loading textiles directly onto canal barges, and now home to the Macclesfield Groundwork Trust. Opened by Brian Redhead in 1986, it is worth a visit as it provides a wealth of information about the area. Here too, the Barge Inn advertises bar meals and a family room for those already seeking refreshment. You are also still walking parallel to the disused railway which, by 1874, operated a large goods yard nearby, importing coal from Poynton Colliery for the mill machinery, and exporting gritstone from the Kerridge quarries.

Leave the canal at the steps leading onto the next bridge (Number 28), which you cross before keeping ahead along a stony track. Turn left along Kerridge Road and then immediately right through a wall-gap which takes you alongside a garden and diagonally up a grassy field. Continue up steep steps beside a wall and then turn left in front of cottages. Huge paving slabs which once echoed to the ring of countless clogs stretch over the next field. The massive network of paved paths in this area dates back to a time when people from all the surrounding villages walked to work in the Bollington mills. Climb over stone steps onto Windmill Lane and, nestling below, the Bulls Head, once a magistrate's court, today serves tasty snacks and Real Ale.

Turn up the hill to the Redway Tavern - a country inn transformed from an end terraced cottage. In the 1920s the owner began selling ale to the local quarrymen at weekends, and probably also sold the produce from his smallholding behind the property. At that time there were six quarries operating on Kerridge, and many part-time ale houses brewed their own beer and sold it to the local community.

Later on the pub became known as the Mad Major after the man who bought the cottage and persuaded his neighbours to sell. Inside, an alcove shows where the second outside door once stood, and pictures of the original building can still be seen on the walls. Nowadays this tavern, which serves meals both at lunchtime and in the evening, is particularly popular with both ramblers and cyclists.

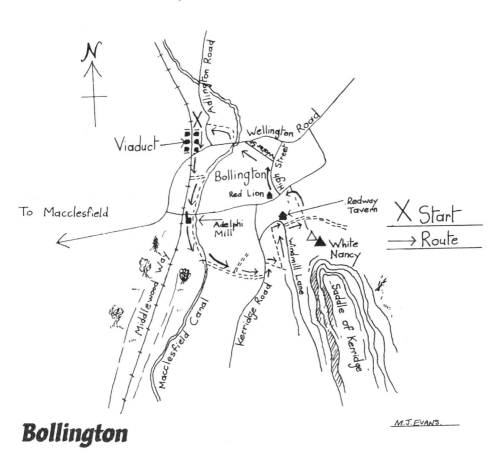

Bollington

M.J.EVANS.

3

Turn left along the far side of the Tavern and follow a footpath signposted up the hill. The view is magnificent as you climb higher, with Bollington's six-mile length spread-eagled below. Many of its buildings are made of Kerridge sandstone quarried from this very hill. After crossing a cattle grid turn sharp right and make a short detour to the summit and White Nancy.

Long before this strange structure was built a beacon stood on the hill here (920 feet above sea level) where a fire could be lit to warn of invasion. The conical sugar-loaf we see today was erected by the Gaskell family of nearby Ingersley Hall to commemorate the Battle of Waterloo in 1815. It stands on the boundary of the parishes of Rainow and Bollington, and was built as a folly where people could picnic. To facilitate this it originally sported a studded, iron door, stone benches and a pedestal table - the slab top of which needed eight horses to drag it up the hill. The name White Nancy is supposed to appertain to one of these horses and, sadly, the structure was reduced to the stout white-walled shape we see today because of vandalism.

Retrace your steps down the hill to the cattle grid. Then continue to descend, following a small section of the Gritstone Trail - a 19-mile, long-distance footpath stretching down the westerly edge of the Pennines from Lyme Park to Rushton Spencer. As its name suggests the Trail covers an area of millstone grit - a very hard form of sandstone ideal for building both houses and roads.

Gaps in two walls lead to steps into a lower field, and you continue along the side of this back to the town. A left turn then takes you to the Red Lion where you turn right down High Street. From here, turn left into Water Street and left again under the massive viaduct - viewed from a different angle this time. Finally, cross over into the park, walking along the side of football and cricket pitches back to the car park.

What a variety crammed into less than two hours - converted railway, cruising canal, Kerridge's notable landmark, spectacular views over Pennines and plain, and the snug cottages, monumental mills and twisting streets of Bollington itself.

HIGH ON THE CLOUD OVER CONGLETON

Distance: **5 to 6 miles**

Undoubtedly Bosley Cloud, rising sharp and sheer 200 feet above the Plain, must afford the grandest view of Congleton and the surrounding countryside. Following the south-easterly borders of the county, this leisurely stroll provides outstanding vistas extending far across both Pennines and Plain; it then provides a bit of ancient history, before ending in the congenial atmosphere of a converted farmhouse.

View from
The Cloud
over the
Cheshire Plain

John Cocks

5

Tucked away on Weathercock Lane in the tiny hamlet of Timbersbrook is a National Trust car park with facilities. Leave it and turn right down the lane, crossing tiny Timbers Brook itself before taking the second right turn up the rough, and often wet, track of Acorn Lane. Cross the road at the top and continue up Gosberryhole Lane, its horrendous hairpins swirling ever higher as you pass ducks on the sheltered pond below Folly Cottage, and then bear left onto National Trust property - a relief to find this local landmark safe from any obliteration by mass development.

Keep left up here, skirting the wood along an insignificant path, but one which affords wide-ranging views over rolling Cheshire pastures. In the far distance, often looming above mist enshrouded fields like a vehicle from outer space, stands the giant, saucer-shaped bowl of Jodrell Bank's famous radio telescope. A massive 250 feet in diameter, it has scanned the heavens continuously since 1957, collecting valuable information for both scientists and weathermen.

Much nearer, almost within touching distance, stands the North Rode railway viaduct: stone for its ten arches was quarried from this very hill, which also produced the foundations for many older Congleton properties. The town itself fans out behind, its origin in Roman times, its bustling weekly market dating from medieval days. From the 13th century it was well-known for the manufacture of leather gloves and 1aces until, four centuries later, Plague wiped out almost the entire population. Silk weaving then took over, and it rivalled Macclesfield for a time, until man-made fibres superseded silk, and a range of light industry added to the town's prosperity.

You have to step gingerly over a tumbling mass of loose boulders to reach The Cloud's lofty summit, and its stupendous view to the easterly hills. The village of Bosley shelters below, cruelly bisected by the Leek road; many will have heard of its tug-of-war team - national champions for a time. Peeping from a copse is its tiny church, 'its quaint and ancient tower older than Agincourt.' Thus Arthur Mee describes it in his chronicle of Cheshire's past. Alongside it a path winds down to the River Dane. Rising on Axe Edge this pretty river meanders placidly through Congleton and Holmes Chapel before joining the Weaver - its largest tributary - at Northwich.

And from Lymford Bridge a country lane rises ever upwards towards the

Cloud, celandine and dog's mercury blanketing its grassy verges. Yet higher still a field path passes stone-built farms perching comfortably on the hillside, and dry stone walls partition the landscape like stitching on a patchwork quilt.

Round the corner the twenty-acre expanse of Bosley Reservoir shines serenely in the Spring sunshine, constructed in 1832 to supply the Macclesfield Canal with water. A conduit descends to this extraordinary waterway. Designed by Thomas Telford, its course seems virtually to ignore all contours as it cuts boldly through the landscape. Opened in 1831, and stretching from Marple to Hall Green, it was one of the last canals to be built before the roistering Age of the Train and, from this vantage point, its course is easily followed over a twenty-arched aqueduct high above the Dane. 2,000 men were employed on the building of this massive structure, each working a fifty-hour week for a wage of 2d an hour and, as if to scorn their effort, the canal then drops through twelve locks - 110 feet in a mile.

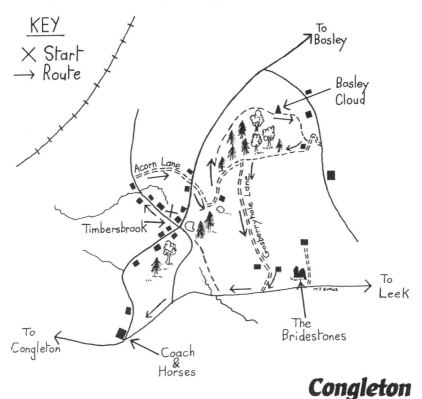

KEY
X Start
→ Route

To Bosley
Bosley Cloud
Acorn Lane
Timbersbrook
Gosberryhole Lane
To Leek
To Congleton
The Bridestones
Coach & Horses

Congleton

Gone are the industrial cargoes of the past; instead, splashes of brightly-coloured pleasure boats move at leisurely pace along its course, some perhaps linking up with both Trent/Mersey and Bridgewater to complete the Cheshire Ring, a canal cruise encircling much of the county.

From the Cloud's trig point, 343 feet above sea level, continue forward along the path; outstanding landmarks are silhouetted against the bleak backdrop of sheep-dotted Pennine fields. The TV and radio transmitter stands high on Croker Hill, overshadowed by Shutlingsloe's triangular peak soaring to its height of 1,659 feet, while the Roaches' ridge reels away into North Staffordshire.

Prehistoric remains at the Bridestones   *John Cocks*

8

After dropping down steep steps turn right up a stony track and, where this bends sharply, cross a stile to follow the wood's edge, beech, pine and bilberry roots jostling hard for prime position. At a junction turn left, then fork left again between banks of purple flowering heather and blazing bracken to rejoin Gosberry Lane, where you turn left once more. A trek along here, and another left fork, brings you onto a mainish road - once a turnpike into the adjoining county.

A glance over your left shoulder takes in the Bridestones, which are worth a visit if you have the energy to walk to them. Etched sharply against a background of rhododendrons, these stark stones are the remains of a prehistoric long barrow dating from 2,300 BC. The only one of its kind with paved forecourt in Britain, it was once much more extensive but, before it became protected, many of its stones were removed, and are now visible in the rockeries of local gardens.

Down the road a right turn over a stile provides a short cut to Tunstall Lane, where you go right back to your car. But, further along, nestling snugly against overlapping hills, is the Coach and Horses, a converted stone-built farm. One of 320 pubs owned by Robinson's family brewery based in Stockport, it serves their best mild beer and full-bodied best bitter, as well as providing home-cooked food in cosy coal-fired rooms. What better way to recharge the batteries ...!

THE DELIGHTS OF DISLEY

Distance: **3 miles**

The tiny township of Disley has long been associated with the great estate of Lyme Park and, travelling along the A6 from Manchester, a glimpse of Lyme Cage may be the first indication that your destination is nigh. An outstanding landmark for miles around, this stolid, square tower has sundials on three sides, and an outstanding history as

The Rams Head dates from Tudor times

John Cocks

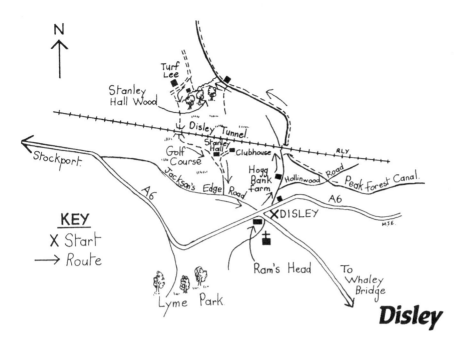

Disley

watchtower, prison, and site for public hangings. Nowadays, it broods above the extensive parkland and Elizabethan hall, where Mary Queen of Scots was once entertained; the whole estate was owned by the Legh family from the 14th century until its acquisition by the National Trust in 1947.

Almost immediately after passing the main entrance to Lyme, the A6 bisects Disley itself, stone-built shops and houses clinging tenaciously to the windswept Pennine slopes. Dominating its centre, and now a Berni Inn, stands the Ram's Head; with its black and white, gabled facade dating from Tudor times it is one of the oldest hostelries in the area. Fronting it is a grassy square, where stands a simple, yet dignified war memorial, and flanking this is a classical fountain, dating from 1823. It provided the citizens of Disley with a reliable water supply until well into this century, never having been known to fail, even in times of severe drought.

Turn right here along the hillside road to Whaley Bridge where, almost immediately on your left, lies a small car park. Opposite its entrance a country lane is worth exploring, from which a cobbled path spirals up to the church. Standing 700 feet above sea level, its hillside foundations are enclosed by an ancient, drystone wall which, moss-covered, rises in places to a height of fifteen feet. Topping the trees the church's four-storeyed

11

tower houses six bells, their resonant notes soaring out over the surrounding countryside.

Dedicated to St. Mary-the-Virgin, the church was founded in 1558 by Sir Piers Legh in memory of his wife. Built as a chantry chapel for Lyme, it also saved Disley folk the trek to Stockport church each Sunday. Sir Piers Legh himself was a distinguished soldier, knight and priest who, although after his wife's untimely death eventually settled at Lyme was, in his early years, associated with Winwick, near Warrington, where well-preserved brass memorials depict both him and his wife. Indeed, it was only after her death that he took Holy Orders and, in memorials both at Winwick and Disley, he is depicted wearing both a priest's vestments and full armour - a rare combination.

The interior of Disley church is light and spacious. The nave, preserved from the original 16th century building, has a splendid, timbered ceiling, graced with gold and silver bosses, crows' feet carvings, and symbolic angels: its dull red background enhances a magnificent centrepiece formed from the crest of the Legh family - a white and gold Ram's Head with blue surround. The stained glass is also worthy of note, the east window depicting scenes from Christ's Passion and dating from the early Renaissance period; on the south wall is a scene showing Mary Magdalene in the garden before the figure of Christ with a spade - symbolic of her mistakenly identifying him as the gardener.

Built into the bank near the church's main door is the memorial garden to the Legh family, and a gravestone in the nave's floor is dedicated to one Joseph Watson, a keeper at Lyme expert in herding deer, and reputed to drink a gallon of beer a day! Perhaps that was the secret of his longevity, for he died in 1753 at the ripe old age of 103.

While visiting the church, stand at the main door and look up to the two-faced vicarage, the visible eastern section only dating from the last century; but hidden round the corner, the long, low walls of rectangular stone which form the westerly facade date back to the 16th century, and inside, huge, carved beams perhaps came from the original Lyme Hall.

Returning to the town and the car park, a cut takes you back to the A6, where you turn right and then left at the Dandy Cock down Hollinwood

Peak Forest Canal, highest navigable waterway in Britain

John Cocks

Road. After passing under the railway bridge bear left again down Hogg Bank Lane, to enjoy breathtaking views over Cobden Edge and Kinder. You soon pass Hogg Bank Farm where the mysterious Hogg Bank Boggart once took up residence; in the 1800s a strange, persistent knocking considerably alarmed the widow who lived there, but whether it was the devil or a disruptive neighbour was never satisfactorily explained.

Keep right along here to cross the Peak Forest Canal by means of a swing bridge. Stretching from Ashton-in-Makerfield to Whaley Bridge, this canal is the highest navigable waterway in Britain and includes both a flight of sixteen locks and a splendid aqueduct over the River Goyt at Marple, as well as two tunnels and a variety of pretty bridges. It was opened in 1800 and, using it, 'fly boats' could complete the journey from Manchester to London in three days, while the Harlequin was a daily packet boat that travelled between Ashton and Marple.

Turn left along the bank, enjoying exhilarating Pennine views as you pass brightly-painted pleasure craft and a lift bridge. You then leave the towpath over Bridge 23, veering right over a stile and down the track into Stanley Hall Wood, where deciduous trees intermingle with rhododendrons and holly. As the path turns away from the canal, gushing water gurgles down a deep cleft, and black-faced sheep may be foraging among the trees. Then bear right to climb above the byres of Turf Lee to a stony track where you turn left along a white fence. Keep right along here, passing an industrial chimney stack - relic of a former mill. Geese may hiss with displeasure as you follow the track to a stile and then the golf course.

Make for the left side of the mound ahead which was formed from earth excavated to make the railway tunnel below. Two miles long, it is the sixth longest railway tunnel in Britain. Along its length ventilation shafts pierce the grassy banks like periscopes, and the gorse-fringed path veers left to Stanley Hall, a 'magpie' building fitting snugly into the sheltering hillside. Turn right away from the clubhouse, perhaps pausing to admire the golfing weather vane on a sturdy, rough-hewn shelter. Then continue along Stanley Hall Lane to Jackson's Edge Road, where you turn right and drop down the hill back to Disley's centre.

FRODSHAM - A MEDIEVAL MARKET TOWN

Distance: **3 miles**

Although the Frodsham of today, occupying a sheltered site below the steep scarp of the Overton Hills, dates from Anglo Saxon times, this area has its roots even deeper in past history. In Neolithic times an iron age hill fort was built at Woodhouse above the present settlement, and the Roman road from Chester to Wilderspool ran close underneath the steep cliffs.

Entering Frodsham along the A56 from Chester, and before crossing the railway line, you can turn right into Castle Park where a children's play area,

A weekly market since medieval days   *John Cocks*

nature trails and an Arts Centre offer enough leisure activites to suit most tastes. The whole estate here was once the home of the Wright family who generously bequeathed it to the town in 1932.

The walk starts by passing the Council Offices (the original family home) followed by the Arts Centre - once the coach house. The family motto, still emblazoned on the clock tower, translates from the Latin as 'a mind which knows what's right', and the clock itself maintains the tradition of being kept three minutes fast. This was started by Edward Wright (an upright Victorian and the property's last owner) who thus eccentrically ensured that he never missed a train from the nearby station! Behind these buildings lies a pretty garden planted by the local Round Table in 1987 and, farther on, the old fire station has been pleasingly converted into sheltered housing.

As you leave the park, cross the road and continue along a footpath beside the railway. Then turn left to the High Street through the yard of the Queen's Head. One of the oldest taverns in the town, it dates back to 1550, being known as the King's Head until the reign of Queen Victoria. In one of the outbuildings, the court leet of the manor of Frodsham was held in an upper room during the 18th century, and a gallows once swung eerily in the wind outside.

Next, turn right along the High Street which is bordered by trees commemorating Queen Victoria's Diamond Jubilee. Extraordinarily wide it is still lined by the cobbles over which stage coaches once rattled. What bone-shaking journeys their passengers must have endured! Every Thursday the street is a-bustle with Frodsham's well-known, weekly market, first authorised in 1215. A miscellany of colourful stalls jostle with one another along the street's length, while vendors of every conceivable commodity - pots and pans, swathes of cloth, vegetables and fruit - compete amicably for custom.

Behind the stalls, mellow red-brick cottages with thatched roofs lie cheek by jowl with magnificent Georgian buildings, and tiny dwellings on sandstone plinths have Roman numerals indented in their timber frames - originally scratched to facilitate the assembly of each beam. Formed from two houses in Regency times, the distinctive Old Hall Hotel dates from the 17th century and has sections of wattle and daub carefully preserved in the dining room walls. Outside in the garden stones mark flood levels from the last century, and a flight of steps leads down into a large stone bath - perhaps an early swimming pool.

Continue along the High Street to the Bear's Paw. Dating back 350 years to Stuart times, its name is derived from the bear baiting that used to take place outside - perhaps ensuring its later popularity as a coaching inn. Almost opposite are fishermen's cottages, reminders of a by-gone age when a small port flourished on the River Weaver at Frodsham Bridge. Early in the 19th century the road here (a turnpike then) was cut through solid rock, local paupers providing much of the labour in return for a pittance of a wage. High above it, and once a Wesleyan Chapel, the library faces steps which you climb, by-passing the Old Cottage. Built into the rock face and dating from 1580, it is one of the oldest properties in the area.

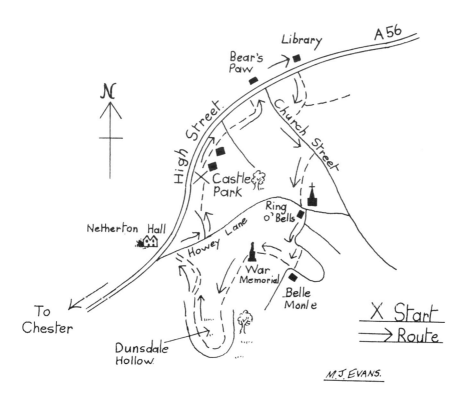

M.J. EVANS.

Frodsham

Continue up a snicket, cross an iron footbridge over the railway, and then veer right down to London Road. On reaching Church Street turn left up the hill, first passing Prospect House (dating from 1781), and then the old Frodsham Police Station (now a private house) on the opposite side of the road. Climb the steps here and continue between high hawthorn hedges to the church.

Built of local red sandstone, Frodsham's Anglican church of St. Lawrence is considered to have the most impressive Norman nave in Cheshire. Shining down upon it from the chancel are the richly burnished hues of a stained glass window dedicated to the praise of famous men: Livingstone, Wren, Galileo, Lister, Handel, Newton, Euclid and Francis Xavier - all these are honoured here.

Continue up Bellemonte Road past the Ring o'Bells, a cosy inn where a warm welcome is further enhanced by an interior of massive beams, a fine heck screen, and an inglenook fireplace. After passing the appropriately-named houses of Hill Side and Rockdale Cottage, you climb into a bluebell wood via steps worn smooth by booted feet. Just before reaching Belle Monte (a Cheshire pub incongruously boasting Samuel Smith's best Yorkshire beer) turn right down an insignificant pathway.

Walking high above the town, keep left at a fork, climbing slightly until the view opens out. At your back the gentler slopes of the Overton Hills flow away from Beacon Hill, where an Armada beacon once stood ready to warn of an unwelcome Spanish invasion. A short scramble from here takes you up to the War Memorial, from which can be seen a breathtaking panorama. The M56, alternately slashing through fields of yellow rape and friesian cattle, transports tankers from Stanlow's oil refineries and Runcorn's chemical plants, which sprawl over much of the remaining land. To the east, the shining arc of Runcorn suspension bridge can be seen, rising 'like a phoenix' over Ship Canal and Mersey.

The way continues below the summit, beside rock cliffs and caves until it joins a gorse-edged path bordering a field. Turn right here and continue, albeit briefly, along The Sandstone Trail; flights of steps facilitate the descent into Dunsdale Hollow although Jacob's Ladder offers a more adventurous route! You soon pass the turreted house of Dunsdale itself as you descend further and keep down Carriage Drive to Netherton Hall.

Originally a farmhouse, it offers tasty meals and a welcome respite for the weary walker! The route then finishes with a right turn up Howey Lane, a left turn down Netherton Drive, and a right fork back into Castle Park.

Today, the sandstone-based settlement of Frodsham stands firm on its hillside site overlooking both Weaver and Mersey. At one time these two large waterways not only provided excellent fishing for the locals (especially salmon) but their receding flood waters also deposited a wide band of rich alluvial soil, which proved ideal for agriculture. Time moves on, however and, although once housing farmers or fishermen, nowadays the town provides a pleasant home environment for workers in the nearby industrial zone.

Distance: **2 miles**

A westerly stone's throw from the M6, sandwiched between the Rivers Dane and Croco to north and south, its easterly border the Manchester to Crewe railway, there hides the tiny township of HolmesChapel. For a long time it consisted only of a church surrounded by a few small cottages, its name 'Holmes Chapel' (pronounced 'chapelle' so I'm told) simply meaning 'the chapel on rising ground'. However, because of its excellent communications - it lies at the junction of five roads - it has developed as a commuter's paradise housing workers travelling as far afield as Manchester and Stoke.

Yet its centre still has an air of unspoilt unworldliness (don't miss the old fashioned stamp machine next to the pillar box) and the tiny shops lining

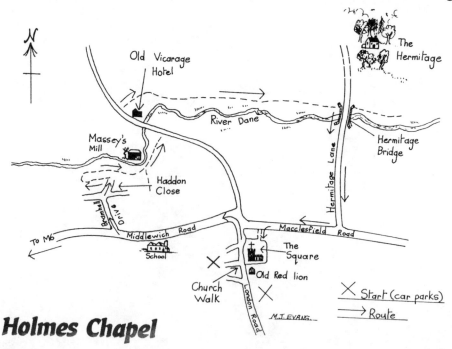

Holmes Chapel

Church Walk are a delight to the eye. Whether you are looking for toys or knitting wool, lace or lilies, you'll find them there, and there are bargains in bedding opposite the church. Another attraction is the ample free parking, either behind these shops or at the precinct further down London Road.

Return to St. Luke's Church past the Old Red Lion which, dating from 1692, is reputedly one of Cheshire's oldest inns. Its gabled windows once overlooked stage coaches which ran daily between London, Liverpool and Birmingham and, in March 1738, its roughcast walls of local brown brick sheltered John Wesley journeying from Oxford to Manchester with two friends. While lodging there Wesley is said to have preached with such fervour that he delayed the meal of fellow guests. Henry Newcombe, another well known Nonconformist, also preached in the town - but in more orthodox surroundings!

Next to the inn, St. Luke's Church with its circular churchyard was perhaps once a pagan shrine. Nowadays, a Glastonbury thorn survives near the porch where Captain Charles Wright is buried - the father of a man who cleared the Dane on horseback. The building itself has a warmly welcoming air and dates back to the start of the 15th century when it was timber framed - brick walls adding extra support three centuries later.

The west tower's rough-hewn walls are composed of red and grey sandstone from Nether Alderley's quarries; pitted and pock-marked by cannon fire they bear the battle scars of the Civil War. The six bells were first hung early in the 18th century and, appropriate today, one is inscribed: 'Heaven Britain bless with plenty and peace'. In bygone times the tenor, described as the draggletail bell, tolled the time for field workers, warned of fire, and signalled services.

The magnificent nave roof with principals of ornamental, shaped timber is supported by four oak pillars and above the aisle hangs a handsome brass candelabra. Dating back to 1713, the church warden's accounts make fascinating reading - a history in miniature - with numerous entries recording payment for 'strange ministers'!

The glorious east window, a fitting memorial to those who died in the First World War, depicts Mary weeping at the foot of the cross surrounded by a warrior, and angels with purple wings. Another window is dedicated to Dr Lionel James Picton OBE. A local character living earlier this century, he visited patients first on horseback, then on a motorbike and finally in a Model T Ford, advocating hard work, rigorous exercise and wholesome food as the best medicine.

Continue north from the church, turning left down Middlewich Road to pass a school before turning right down Bramhall Drive. Veer right again down Haddon Close, then loop left and right through a kissing gate and down a footpath. Keep ahead, climbing a stile and following the River Dane past a herd of goats to the thunderous weir. On the opposite bank are bulky buildings now housing Massey's animal foodstuffs; the place was first a mill, then a forge, then a flour mill, and is still known by older locals as Massey's Mill.

Leave the field over an awkward stile by the gate and turn left over the low-arched bridge built in 1800. Pass the Old Vicarage Hotel - once the parson's home - before turning right through a plant nursery. Here, a stile takes you into a field where you bear right to cross two more stiles - the second bearing the daunting notice 'Bull in Field'. Don't worry, you can always escape into the river as you follow its twisting course to a stile by an ash!

From here one gets an excellent view of Robert Stephenson's splendid, 23-arched railway viaduct. The largest on the Manchester-Crewe line it was completed in 1841, each symmetrical bow soaring in a 63-foot span from the flat, valley floor.

Built on a hermit's refuge, The Hermitage can be glimpsed through a shroud of trees as you reach Hermitage Lane. Although now converted into three properties, the original house dated from the 13th century and was once owned by the Winnington family, staunch Royalists and Catholics. The Hermit's Room was then a secret chapel with a priest's hole below. When, during the Second World War, the place was requisitioned for the Services, one WAAF was far more terrified of a night spent in that room than of any of Hitler's bombing raids!

As you turn right over Hermitage Bridge, TBH (the builder's initials) and the date (1828) can be deciphered among the graffiti-garnished stonework. Keep ahead to Fine Art Wallcoverings, set up early this century on the site of another old mill. In an adjacent house the golfer Henry Cotton was born. Turn right here, passing an agricultural engineering business (a reminder that this has always been farming country), and Mandeville's - a family bakery established early this century, which produces mouth-watering fare.

Finally, turn left down a short snicket into The Square, noticing numbers 3 and 5 - the only two dwelling houses in the town to survive a horrific and sudden fire one morning in July 1753. Built early in the 18th century as part of a dormer terrace, the recessed sash windows have glazing bars and prominent keystones to their heads, and they epitomise the heart of this busy little town ensconced so snugly in the Cheshire Plain.

MIDDLEWICH - A SALT TOWN

Distance: **3 to 4 miles**

Many people would feel that Ormerod got it right when he wrote that Cheshire was a 'land of beauty and brine'.

Way back in pre-history the Cheshire Plain was once a lagoon fed by the sea, a warmer climate then evaporating the sea water and leaving behind that precious commodity - salt. It was discovered here even before Roman times, but they introduced its collection in metal pans, a process only recently superseded by the vacuum method.

Northwich, Nantwich and Middlewich - the three 'wiches' - which, together with Winsford, make up the salt towns of Cheshire. As its name implies,

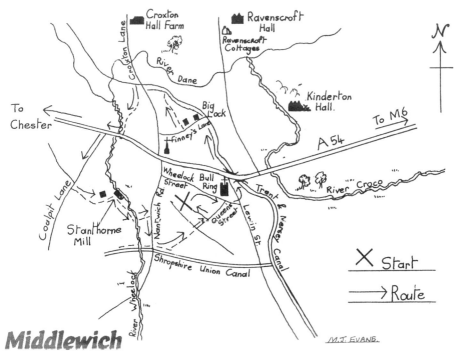

Middlewich was the linchpin, and indeed boasted two brine springs (Great Seth and Little Seth), whereas both Northwich and Nantwich had only one apiece.

The first salt works was even started here and, in 1605, the annual value of local salt amounted to over £4,000 - then a considerable sum. Later, in the 19th century, Henry Seddon advertised seven different types of salt: cheese salt, butter salt, table salt, curing salt (for hams and bacon),

The White Bear - sorely in need of a face-lift!   *John Cocks*

agricultural salt, rock salt (for horses and cattle), and bay salt (for brine baths). Uncouth women were often employed in the salt industry and their choice language gave rise to the well-known Cheshire saying, 'She swears like a wych-waller!'

The car park behind Gateway is free even on Tuesdays when it accommodates a bustling market. From it a path drops down to Wheelock Street, turning right to pass the White Bear's sadly decrepit frontage; in Victorian times a coaching inn of some importance, an archway leads into Lady Anne's Court, where cobbles and converted stabling offer a glimpse of the past.

Middlewich's quaint and uneven streets remain much as they were a century ago when Wakes Week took place each year and, as you drop down to the Bull Ring, you can almost imagine the vivid scene: donkey and smock races, sword swallowers, blackamoors, and bear baiting when Middlewich's bear, Old Nell, was a major attraction. Often a mixture of sacred and secular, the following local rhyme aptly portrays this jolly celebration:

> *Drencht in ale or drowned in beere;*
> *Happy rusticks best content*
> *With the cheapest merriment;*
> *And possess no other feare*
> *Than to want the Wake next yeare!*

Almost aloof on its knoll stands the church of St. Michael and All Angels. Fragments of stone carved with a wolf's head (crest of Hugh Lupus, first Earl of Chester) lie in the churchyard below the Norman tower, which sports the Venables' coat of arms. Its macabre crest depicts the legend that a dragon, in the act of devouring a child, was slain by Thomas Venables.

The family's roots are impressive. Gilbert de Venables, cousin of William the Conqueror, after fighting at Hastings was rewarded with the Baronetcy of Kinderton and extensive property around mid-Cheshire. The family was ferociously split during the Wars of the Roses; Hugh, baron at the time, upholding the Lancaster cause, while his brother, Richard, supported the House of York.

Although the family was loyal to the crown throughout the Civil War, marks of battle can still be seen in the church walls from when Sir William

The church's
Norman tower
guards the
Trent & Mersey
Canal

John Cocks

Brereton's army routed the Royalist troops. Later, vengeance was taken when Lord Byron and an Irish army defeated Brereton, killing over 200 Roundheads in Booth Lane. Kinderton Hall, lying to the east, was well-fortified to house goods and cattle for the Royalists throughout these unsettled years. Later, it became the home of Elias Ashmole, a local antiquary.

Perpendicular in style, the church was restored during the 19th century and inside, pillars adorned by leaves, flowers and grotesque faces, are reflected by some beautiful stained glass. There are exquisite carvings too of the Annunciation, the Nativity and Baptism of Christ, and the Last Supper, as well as a Jacobean poor box.

Continue past the King's Arms - once a stop for stage coaches when both a fanfare of trumpets and a gun salute heralded the mail's arrival each day. You soon reach Leadsmithy Street which takes its name from the lead pans manufactured and repaired there for salt collection. To the right it becomes Lewin Street, the town's oldest thoroughfare, which bears a Saxon name meaning 'landowner': numbers 33 and 33a are prime examples of black-and-white cottages.

Cross the road here: bear left, then almost immediately right beside Wharf Cottage to James Brindley's Trent & Mersey Canal - finally completed in 1777 after his death. Turn left along the towpath, soon passing tall, modern housing of an unusual, almost-Dutch design. Strangely in keeping with the canalside scene, and with paintwork of cream and misty blue, they offer a refreshing change from the ubiquitous mock Tudor so prevalent at present. At the Big Lock, turn left beside the Victorian inn to Finney's Lane. Then, after passing British Crepe, go right along a snicket bordering untidy fields.

The cemetery's spire stands high above the surrounding scene. One of its first monuments, placed near the entrance, was a plinth to the Cooke family of Brierley Hulme Farm. The parents, four young children, and a nanny aged only twelve, all perished in a horrendous fire on a Saturday in November 1867. Only fragments of bone and a lady's gold ring were found in the ashes, the tragedy being commemorated in verse by a Knutsford poet. A somewhat more light-hearted epitaph in the parish churchyard reads: *Some have children, some have none,*
But here lies the mother of twenty-one.   Heaven forbid!

Leaving thoughts of death behind, keep parallel with back gardens until you veer right back to the canal. Roach, gudgeon and perch abound underneath the silent surface, while the distance between Shardlow and Preston Brook is proclaimed on iron signposts unique to this canal.

To the north-east lies Ravenscroft Hall. Built in Greek Ionic style, its name is thought to originate from ravens which nested in the tall trees during Roman times. Near its entrance stand Ravenscroft Cottages - estate houses erected in Victoria's reign for coachman and gardener. Ahead, the distinctive black-and white eaves of Croxton Hall Farm stand high on the hillside. One of the earliest places to make Cheshire cheese, with a product once deemed the world's best.

Croxton Lane passes over the canal at Bridge 173. Entering Middlewich along this road you pass Croxton Lane Villas. Comprising three storeys and a cellar, in Victorian and Edwardian times they were roomy enough to house the large familes of doctors, teachers, and industrialists plus a live-in maid.

After a few yards, a muddy lane bears off at right angles from the canal. Go down it, then through an area of land clearance to reach the River Wheelock via a narrow, nettle-edged footpath. Turn left along its banks, then right at the main road and almost immediately left again down Coalpit Lane. After passing Mill Farm and Birch Lane turn left over a cattle grid to Stanthorne Mill.

Cattle, sheep, and sleekly-groomed horses, followed by a crop of beet, indicate mixed farming as you walk to Stanthorne Mill House and the converted mill. Then continue along a footpath to the weir where a foaming torrent roars in thunderous tumult, before you ascend, via Mill Lane, to Nantwich Road.

Turn right from here to the aqueduct where you climb up a flight of steep steps and bear left along the Shropshire Union Canal. This branch, opening in 1833, carried coal from the Midlands to mid-Cheshire for the salt industry, transporting clay on the return journey. Opposite the fourth bungalow turn left down a snicket which runs past school playing fields to St. Ann's Road. Cross this and continue ahead down King Edward Street and Queen Street back to the car park. Originally Dog Lane, Queen Street was renamed during Queen Victoria's reign when the King's Head also became the Queen's Head for a while.

Twenty miles from Chester, and once only second in importance to it, Middlewich's roots lie even deeper in the past. Flints and axe heads from the Stone Age, and bronze implements, have provided ample evidence that prehistoric man settled in the vicinity, and numerous Roman remains are on display in the local library.

Condate (Middlewich's Roman name) means 'a joining' and seven Roman roads converged nearby at Kinderton, one of which, King Street, was the main route to Manchester and the north. Besides being at the junction of two canals and on a main railway line, the town is also at the confluence of three lovely rivers - the Croco, the Wheelock and the Dane, which thread their way through the gently undulating countryside.

For these reasons alone it is surprising that Middlewich has remained so tiny, this mid-Cheshire town with its rows of terraced cottages which line the higgledy-piggledy streets almost offering obeisance to the imposing, hilltop church.

Cheers! at the King's Lock   *John Cocks*

NESTON AND LITTLE NESTON

Distance: **3 to 4 miles**

S o much is written about Parkgate, once a sea front resort and now boasting four pubs along its short length, that Neston itself seems almost to take a back seat. Yet there is much to commend both it and the adjoining community of Little Neston, as they nestle in Parkgate's affluent hinterland.

Built on solid sandstone, as were many Wirral communities, there has been a settlement here since Saxon times; the word Neston means 'town by the headland', although this was long ago eroded away by high tides. The town

Neston

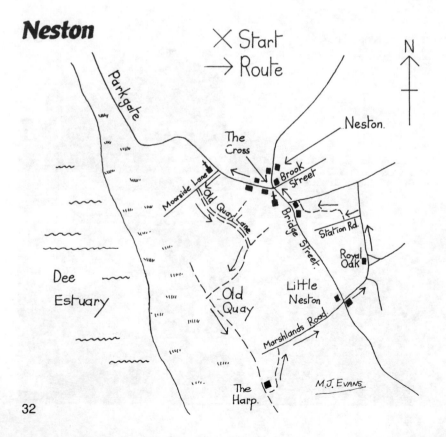

The Cross at Neston's busy centre   *John Cocks*

originated as an agricultural settlement and market for the surrounding area
and then, from the Middle Ages until the mid-1900s developed both as a
commercial centre and as a seaport for Ireland. In fact, Neston was for
many years the largest town on The Wirral, until the Dee's extensive silting
diverted ships around the headland into Liverpool's deepwater estuary,
which left the area a relative backwater.

Parking is no problem. When you reach The Cross in Neston's centre, turn
down Brook Street where car parks branch off on either side of the road.
A few strides bring you back to The Cross, where a fountain of Scottish
granite stands as a memorial to Christopher Bushell. Liverpool wine
merchant, chairman of local magistrates and generous benefactor to
charity, his home was nearby at Hinderton Hall, and he was responsible for
sinking a public well at The Cross in 1865 - the fountain later being built
above this in recognition of his work in the community.

Proceed along Parkgate Road. As children, some older citizens can remember skipping down here to play on Parkgate's golden sands! The splendid sundial set high into the Georgian facade of Vine House is soon passed. This house was, for many years, home of the local doctor, and another feature of it is the crinkle-crankle wall which surrounds two sides of the back garden - a rarity found mostly in East Anglia.

Further down the road a wall plaque denotes where John Wesley preached on 1st April 1762 while waiting for a favourable wind to Ireland. The service started at 5 a.m. (dedication indeed) and was abruptly cut short when news came that his boat would sail within the hour. The tiny chapel that once stood here was first converted into stables, and then demolished early this century. Next, turn left down Moorside Lane, where a Victorian post box set snugly into the wall faces the more noticeable bulk of the United Reformed Church; its architect, Frederick Doyle, was also responsible for the re-building of the present parish church during the last century.

You soon walk over the top of the Wirral Way, now a footpath stretching for twelve miles from Hooton to West Kirby. This now defunct railway line from Chester to Birkenhead displaced Neston's thrice-weekly coach service to London in the 1800s, but was then axed itself in the Beeching cuts. The line here was dynamited through solid sandstone rock: the dank walls, 25 feet high in places, now form a secluded place rarely disturbed other than by booted ramblers, a slinking fox, or perhaps the flutterings of a tiny wren.

Turn left again down Old Quay Lane, where an eerie hush descends over the flat, extensive marshlands which reach to the now-diminutive Dee, and where, on the Welsh shore, triangular summits peak above mist-shrouded hills. Bordering the lane, brambles and bracken fight in glorious profusion for supremacy over willowherb, thistle, bindweed, nettle and dock, and Deeside Cottage may well once have stood on the river's banks.

Where the road veers right keep ahead through a rusted iron kissing gate; the path, bounded at first by high hawthorn hedgerows, eventually bears right over a field. Continue alongside a blackthorn hedge topped by hawthorn, until a single sycamore heralds the spot where bramble and elder ramble over crumbling walls as a once-busy quayside degenerates back to nature. New Quay was its name in 1545 and it survived an invasion scare

34

during Armada year when a Spanish fleet comprising 700 ships nearly landed here.

In more peaceful past times you can imagine the fishermen unloading catches of shrimps, crabs and lobsters, their wives waiting patiently to fill their donkey-drawn cart. Smugglers too once docked here with illegal assignments of tea, tobacco and spirits, and Nelson is reputed to have used the wharf when keeping secret trysts with the desirable Lady Hamilton! Only a pile of rubble remains to denote the Old Quay House with its intriguing past - first a customs' house, then a prison for runaway servants, and finally a private dwelling.

Continue forward through a sparse, low-lying copse of hawthorn and sycamore where cattle find meagre shelter from the biting winter winds whipping across the estuary. Concrete high-rise buildings signal Flint on the opposite shore as you climb over solid sandstone steps and turn left along the dry ground adjacent to the marsh. Now owned by the RSPB this perfect wild-life sanctuary is home to the natterjack toad, to sundry bog-loving plants, to kestrels, sparrowhawks and short-eared owls, plus a myriad of other birds.

Soon the rushes rustling and soughing in the chilly breeze give way to slag heaps and runnels, their blackened slopes partly obliterated by the temerity of gorse and broom. Further on stand the old colliery offices of the local mine - now a private dwelling. Denhall Colliery was opened here in 1760 by Sir John Stanley of Hooton Hall, but it proved a difficult mine to work, only producing poor-grade coal, most of which was exported to Ireland and North Wales.

Tunnels were excavated under the estuary for more than a mile, and coal was transported along two subterranean canals to the shafts. Four narrow, flat-bottomed barges were roped together to form a train, which the miners propelled by lying on the coal and pushing their feet against the roof. Many of the miners themselves originated from Lancashire, Staffordshire and North Wales, and the terraces of Seven Row and New Street which lie behind the pub were built to house the colliers and their families.

Old farm buildings give way to modern bungalows before The Harp takes you back to the past. A property dating back to 1711, and a pub from the middle of the 19th century, it is still very much a locals' haunt (always a worthy recommendation) and it serves home-made food and enough Real Ale to tempt any thirsty traveller. At one time it was one of only two beer houses in the area, the other being the Durham Ox - now defunct. Run by Ray and June Oldfield (local folk who also run the Coach & Horses nearby) it has recently been sympathetically refurbished; the original tiny rooms, their ceilings still crossed by blackened beams, are enhanced by pictures and mementoes from a long-gone mining heyday.

A sheltered garden lies at the side, and a patio now overlooks the silted shoreline. In fact, although The Harp is still liable to occasional flooding, at one time the Dee came right to its door. Today, however, a nearby grassy sward sheltered by trees forms an ideal family picnic spot or a place to enjoy the pub's home-made ice cream. Tumbling down from here are massive sandstone slabs, which once formed the wall of Denhall Quay and now end abruptly where an insignificant runnel gently meanders along - an apology for the once mighty Dee.

Walk up the side of the pub to Orchard Drive, turning left and then right into Marshlands Road, and passing Colliery Green Drive and Court - evocative names from earlier times. Then walk under the railway bridge passing St. Michael's New Community Church before continuing up Bull Hill to turn left into Town Lane. Here, the Royal Oak, a thatch-roofed pub until decimated by fire, faces The Green where the peddlar Cheap Jack spread out his wares in days long gone.

Keep down Mellock Lane until, after passing a school complex, the road rises and you turn left again down Station Road. You soon turn right down a snicket and then can wander down through pretty gardens or a children's play area to the far end where a left turn under the railway takes you to Bridge Street.

Turn right here to reach the parish church with its Norman tower, where the bell ringers were paid £1 (a princely sum) to celebrate Nelson's victory at Waterloo. Records also show that Lady Hamilton, born at Ness and daughter of the village blacksmith, was baptised here in 1765.

Before retracing your steps from The Cross to the car park, it is worth reflecting on another notable feature of which Neston is justifiably proud - its Ladies' Day parade. The Neston Female Friendly Society was founded in 1814. The first society to be formed for the mutual self-help of women, now it is the only one still to survive, and women from many walks of life proudly parade here each year on the first Thursday in June. It is difficult to decide whether the appointment of a male secretary is simply an incongruity or a small concession to the opposite sex!

The service started at 5 a.m. - dedication indeed!

John Cocks

JOHN WESLEY
PREACHED IN THE
SMALL HOUSE CHAPEL
NEAR THIS SITE
ON 1ST APRIL 1762

RUNCORN: NEW TOWN WITH OLD ROOTS

Distance: **2 miles**

Have *you* visited Runcorn recently to sample its pure, salt waters and fine, fresh air?' Not a likely question nowadays, but in the last century Runcorn (then known as Montpelier) was noted as a spa town with an invigorating atmosphere and glorious views.

The settlement here, however, goes back much further into history. In 916AD Aethelfleda, King Alfred's daughter, visited its fort - built to withstand ferocious Danish raids, together with others at Eddisbury and Thelwall. A ferry too has crossed the Mersey at Runcorn Gap since the 12th century when it was used chiefly by pilgrims visiting the shrine of St. Werburgh in Chester: nearby Norton Priory was also established then. In

All Saints' Church
with walls
of local stone

John Cocks

Old Runcorn

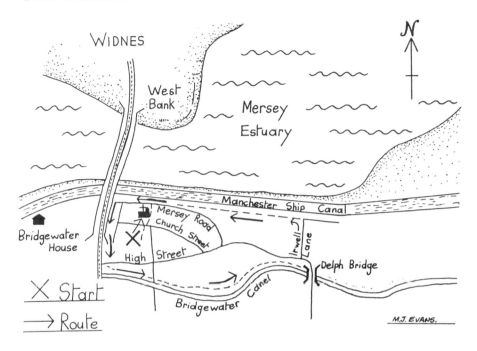

the Middle Ages there was fishing and milling, a weekly market and two annual fairs. Finally, during the turbulent Civil War years Runcorn Castle was demolished by Cromwell.

Since then Runcorn's population has increased dramatically, from around 800 in 1780 to well over 70,000 in the New Town of today. Designated a New Town to rehouse Liverpudlians in 1964 it was the first to be grafted onto an existing community, and the old town now forms a tiny oasis in a desert of new development. The Shopping City alone covers 13 acres, with parking for 300 cars; yet, although traffic-free and undercover, it remains a rather soulless white elephant. Another innovation was the purpose-built, figure-of-eight Expressway along which buses weave spasmodically around the town.

Another reason for the dramatic rise in the population of both Widnes and Runcorn has been the growth of chemical works here. In a recent Gallup Poll the Industry, despite providing many local jobs, was still heavily criticised for air pollution, and considerable anxiety was also expressed about the storage, use and transportation of toxic waste from the plants. A further insidious form of pollution which pervades Old Runcorn Town and its environs is the litter problem which mars what should be a delightful stroll through working class history. Directions are easy to follow using the plethora of pubs - sturdy, workingmen's citadels. A secluded car park stands outside The Wellington, from which you can drop down to All Saints Church.

A church has stood on this site from early times; the first, built by Queen Aethelfleda, was followed by another dedicated to St. Bertelin. After further dedications to St. Mary and St. Bartholomew the title of All Saints seems particularly appropriate for the present building, designed last century by Anthony Salvin. With walls of warm, pink, Runcorn sandstone it cost only £9,000 to build, both tower and spire soaring above the Mersey.

Over the Manchester Ship Canal to Runcorn - old and new   *John Cocks*

At the time of its inception local families rented pews, those on the south side of the aisle costing the princely sum of £2 per annum. Also inside are altar rails of alabaster and an oaken pulpit, its carved panels depicting Christ in three guises: Light of the World, Good Shepherd, and Sower. In the churchyard's south-east corner stands a Manweb substation. Four-square and squat, this building once housed the local hearse. Before funeral directors came into existence a joiner would make the coffin and horses from a nearby farm would head the procession.

Take the north-east exit from the churchyard and adjacent stand Belvedere, and Clarence Terrace. Built in 1831 they once housed visitors coming to sample the fresh air and fine views. One can imagine the ladies in their finery parading along the promenade here which bordered the Mersey prior to the building of both the Ship Canal and Mersey Road. To your right is a green plaque attached to the old river wall which commemorates the opening of Mersey Road in March 1924 - a time of acute unemployment.

Wide, exhilarating views stretch over the water to West Bank and Fiddler's Ferry as you turn left. In 1868 James Brindley, brilliant engineer of the Bridgewater Canal, first proposed a bridge here but it was not until 1905 that the Transporter Bridge, or the Magnificent Monstrosity as it was affectionately nicknamed, was opened. You pass its site. It was replaced in 1961 by the vast, graceful arc of today's suspension bridge. Despite accommodating three lanes of traffic this soon became woefully inadequate, especially during peak times and, in 1975 it was widened to four lanes plus a cantilevered footpath. Now known officially as the Silver Jubilee Bridge it was only closed for one day during all the alterations. Behind it, stone pillars support the battlemented approaches of the older, iron railway bridge.

Continue along South Bank terrace. Then turn left, walking under the suspension bridge and alongside serried rows of back-to-back terraces. A short tunnel to the left of The Devonshire public house brings you to Waterloo Bridge and the termination of the Bridgewater Canal. The bridge's prettily designed wrought ironwork is painted grey and white and Bridgewater House still stands incongruously in dockland nearby. In its Georgian elegance resided the Duke of Bridgewater and James Brindley (creators of the Canal) while overseeing the staircase of locks which once stood here. Made of locally quarried sandstone, the canal was completed in 1776 and facilitated the transportation of coal from Worsley, near Manchester, to the Mersey estuary.

Turn left along the towpath where narrow boats, converted for leisure use, line each bank nose-to-tail and you soon reach Doctor's Bridge. A ship and faded plaque just visible in the stonework, commemorate its opening in 1878 - its name evolving because several doctors practised on the High Street here. A tangled bushy mass on the opposite bank serves as a reminder that Runcorn's name may originate from the latin word *runcare* meaning *a place over-run with brambles and briars*.

Leave the canal at the Egerton Arms and Delph Bridge, dropping down Irwell Lane to cross the Expressway. When you can continue no farther turn left through a litter-strewn snicket which takes you along to the Old Quay. This was the original wharf of the Old Quay Canal which, as part of the Mersey & Irwell Navigation system, connected Runcorn with Latchford for a time, and its docks lined with workshops are still plainly visible.

Here too is the site of Runcorn's first swimming baths. Built in 1822, salt water from the unpolluted Mersey filled the two pools - segregated bathing of course! And that brings us back full circle with Runcorn renowned as a health resort, ignorant of the chemical smells and unsightly litter which later were to pervade the 20th century.

The suspension bridge - once Europe's largest - soars above the town   *John Cocks*

SAXON CROSSES AT SANDBACH

Distance: **1 to 2 miles**

T o my way of thinking no visit to Sandbach is complete without a look at its famous Saxon crosses and a visit to its equally well known Thursday market. This latter, dating back to Elizabethan times, is greatly enhanced by the presence of Paul on the china stall whose witty and occasionally ribald repartee has to be heard to be believed. He certainly draws a fascinated crowd, some of whom (the good catchers) even collect 'somat for nowt' as they say in Yorkshire!

If visiting the town on market day you may have to park in one of the side streets but at any other time the market area provides free parking. This triangular space acquired its ancient name of Scots Common during the English Civil War, when the Scots, retreating after the Battle of Worcester, rested here. The townspeople, fearing a rout similar to that at Barthomley, ferociously attacked them, imprisoning so many in the church that next day's Sunday services had to be held outside.

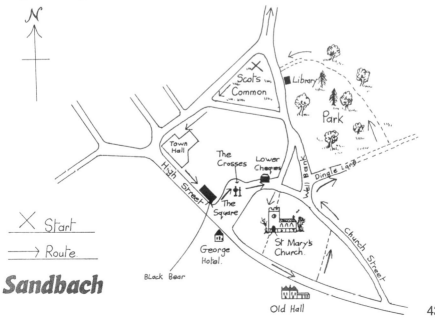

Market Day beneath the fine Town Hall

John Cocks

At the far end of the market place one can see the Town Hall's distinctive bell tower which houses the town's former fire bell. Make for this through the market hall and, on emerging onto High Street turn to see statues of Bigot, the first Norman to hold Sandbach, and Sir Randolph Crewe, whose heraldic coat of arms also decorates the doorway.

Then turn left down the High Street to the Black Bear. Sandbach's only thatched building, it dates back to 1634 and bear baiting outside certainly used to increase its trade. Keeping left over the The Square's cobbles brings you to the famous Sandbach Crosses. Of Saxon antiquity, they are thought to originate from about 653AD when Paeda, son of Mercia's king, was converted to Christianity while resting here with his new bride.

Despite the ravages of time and weather, the taller cross still depicts the main events in the life of Christ - the Annunciation, Nativity, Passion and Crucifixion - while the shorter one shows scenes from Paeda's own journeyings. Completely demolished in the 17th century, during a period of Puritan zeal, we have Ormerod to thank for recovering their pieces from all sorts of strange places, even as far afield as Utkinton Hall and Oulton Park, then restoring them to their former glory. Older citizens of today can remember playing on the surrounding steps, unconcerned by the proximity of priceless antiquity.

Continue to the Lower Chequers. A mounting block still evident outside, this is the oldest building in the town, dating back to 1570. Its unusual name originated from a time when a former landlord owned a chequered board to help illiterate locals count their money - an early abacus perhaps.

Turn right through the church gates and walk under the tower's unusual archway. This public right-of-way is another rarity - a similar example of which can only be found at Wrotham in Kent. The church, which is lovingly swept and polished, is always open on market days and is worth a visit. Two fonts stand either side of the main aisle: one of stone dating from the last century is inscribed with an anacrostic, while a much earlier one was rediscovered in a cottage garden and dates back to 1200 - when the first church was built on this site.

As you leave the churchyard by the south gate far to your right stands The George, once a very busy coaching inn - a daily stop for the London stage coach, and The Rocket travelling between Liverpool and Birmingham. However, you turn left towards the Old Hall Hotel, a magnificent 17th century building, originally square until the long wing was added. Inside are oak panels, secret doors, Jacobean fireplaces, and even a ghost - of course! This one is said to be a grey lady, perhaps sadly searching for a baby whose skeleton was found behind oak panelling in the dining room.

Opposite the hotel drop down steps, at the bottom of which is a water spout and trough of clear water. Continue under the church wall along Front Street, turning left up Church Street for a short way before veering right down Well Bank and right again into Dingle Lane. Keep forward along here until a left turn takes you into the town's park, where a peaceful stroll along its pathways ends this walk. A grove of sycamores commemorates the

Queen Mum's 80th birthday in 1980, and at the exit is a stone memorial to Charles Latham, a much-loved local physician during the last century.

Sandbach should not only be noted for its Saxon crosses but also for its miscellany of 17th century, half-timbered dwellings, which are unexpectedly discovered round every corner - delightful relics of Tudor England. And this short stroll through one of Cheshire's most attractive towns really is enhanced by the Thursday market - where there's always the chance of a bargain ...!

Butchery before the Saxon crosses! *John Cocks*

TARPORLEY - A TRADING POST

Distance: **3 miles**

John Cocks

Apear wood near a hill called Torr', thus runs the most favoured explanation of the name 'Tarporley', a village that has always formed a nucleus for the surrounding hamlets. Nearby, the gigantic footprints of an ancient dinosaur were once discovered deeply embedded in the soft sandstone rock, and it was most probably a settlement as far back as Roman times.

More recently, during the Civil War years, several skirmishes took place in the district: helmets and armour from those troubled times lie today in the parish church. From medieval times until the recent by-pass was built, Tarporley has not only straddled the main road from Chester to Nantwich, but has also developed around the junction for the north-south route down from Warrington.

Turning off the by-pass north of the village you pass the Portal estate. Although hidden from the road it is dominated by a grand mock Tudor mansion which took five years to build at the beginning of this century, and

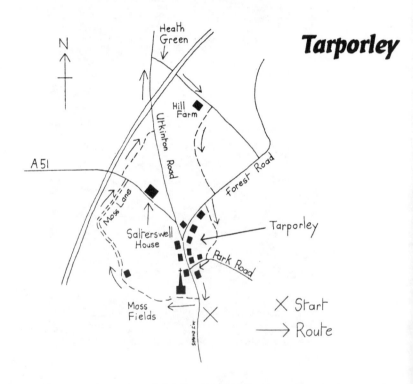

it houses a glorious collection of 16th century Swiss stained glass and a stone Jacobean chimney piece. You then drop down into Tarporley itself, turning left to pass Georgian terraces before reaching the far end of the shopping street.

Public parking is allowed in the car park behind the British Legion during the day and, as over seven miles of public footpaths run in and around the village, a walk is easy to plan. Turn right up the High Street to the church, rather grandly dedicated to St. Helen, mother of the Roman Emperor Constantine. On the way look out for the modest manor house. Perhaps the smallest in the country, it was built in 1586 by Ralph Done, a prominent local landowner, and the family's coat of arms can still be seen below one of its half-timbered eaves.

Across the road is the old Fire Station. Procuring its first fire engine in 1866, the Brigade was established three years later, and the firemen had to live less than two minutes' walk away. In 1929 the original horse-drawn vehicle was replaced by a motor vehicle - the only one in the whole country to be driven by a woman. (Obviously Tarporley folk believed in Women's Lib. long before it came into vogue nationally!) From its inception Tarporley's Fire Brigade has served all the surrounding area, and one officer sadly lost his life while fighting the disastrous fire at Oulton Hall.

Ancient milestone *John Cocks*

```
TO          TO
Tarvin 5M  Nantwich 9M
Chester 10  Woore   18
           Stone    30
           London  172


       Tarporley
       Township
```

Turn left walking through Church Walk to the cemetery where, beside the church, stands a sundial of blackened stone. Brought here from Utkinton Hall in 1932 and dedicated to a much-loved Vicar, its sandstone plinth once may well have formed the base for an ancient village cross. West of the church stands the Done Room. Dorothy Done had it built and, in 1666, endowed with £20 per year from the same family, it became Tarporley's first school. For many years the boys were educated there free while the girls had to pay 1d per week - an injustice unlikely to be tolerated today!

At the bottom of the graveyard walk through an iron kissing gate and then keep diagonally right over the Moss Fields, a grassy but

49

well-trodden path leading you to a cottage and a left-hand stile. Negotiate it and walk down the side of the next field for a short way until you cross another stile and turn right through a secluded extension to the cottage's pretty garden. Then continue along the track leading away from this attractive spot.

You soon walk beside the by-pass along Moss Lane, from where you have a good view of Salterswell House. The well still stands in the wall there, where salters from Nantwich stopped to water their laden pack horses. The impressive Georgian house was owned by the Done family for many years,

Tarporley Church - grandly dedicated to St. Helen, mother of
Constantine the Great   *John Cocks*

and one occupant, Richard Done, endeared himself to the village children on fair days by manoeuvring his horse and trap to knock over the gingerbread stall. Replete children wandered home that night, not a few suffering from a surfeit of the tasty goodies, and the miscreant always recompensed the stall holder in full for his lost trade.

Cross the A51 here and keep ahead down a grassy path below the level of the bypass; then continue over loose stones until you climb up to Utkinton Road. Here turn left, crossing above the new road before going right down Heath Green. Cross back over the busy thoroughfare with care and continue down a country lane which passes through the area known as Ash Hill. At the far side of Hill Farm turn right over a stile and walk along the hedge to steep stone steps which take you down into the next field. Then keep forward to climb over a stile in the far left-hand corner. Turn left here and keep in this direction to Forest Road where you turn right.

Ahead, shining gas lamp standards patrol down the village street, but you turn left down a tiny passageway before the wagon houses. These were once a row of stables with the wagoner's house at the end, where flour from the mills at Huxley, or cheese from the local farms would be unladen from pack horses, the goods then being transferred to wagons and sent to Manchester and Warrington for sale. Imports too which came into the country via Birkenhead were also sent on to Manchester from here.

Continue along this passage, the pervasive smell of musty earth permeating the atmosphere as you pass beneath trees along to Richmond Manse and Park Road. Here a right turn takes you back to the High Street. Opposite, stands the Rising Sun, owned by the Woodward family for many years when, during Race Week it was renowned for its salty communal pie - heavily seasoned to induce a great thirst! The same family also owned the saddler's next door, at a time when Tarporley was well endowed with horsy trades - saddlers, blacksmiths and wheelwrights. Indeed, horse racing was once a popular sport in the area and, in 1930, Tarporley was the first English race course to operate a Tote.

Lower down the street lies the now-secluded Market Court, which once housed the Parish bread oven. Dough left by children on their way to morning school was baked there, then collected on their way home, after which the less conscientious would liven up their journey by using the round loaves as footballs!

It would be hard to miss the grand facade of the Swan Hotel, a building which dates back to 1769 and was once an important coaching inn on the route from London and the Midlands to Chester and Holyhead. It also became the headquarters of the Tarporley Hunt Club which was founded in 1762 by nine of the young local gentry 'purely to enjoy the pleasures of the chase'. Thereafter, the local hunt took place in November each year and some time after its inception a Hunt Room holding 150 people became established upstairs. In it a carved oak chair donated by the Duke of Westminster still stands alongside another fashioned by a local carpenter.

On the eastern slopes of the Gowy Valley, sheltered to the north and west by low, sandstone hills, Tarporley as we know it developed as a typical 'street village', but it has since become a bustling local centre serving the surrounding tiny hamlets. Although still a hive of activity it is now mercifully reprieved from through traffic by the welcome by-pass, and its inhabitants can thankfully visit the thriving shops which line both sides of the road without negotiating an incessant stream of impatient drivers and noxious fumes.

The Done family's coat-of-arms nestles in the eaves
of Tarporley's tiny manor house   *John Cocks*

TO WEST KIRBY VIA THE WIRRAL WAY

Distance: **6 miles**

I f you believe in luck try standing in an unknown town with a bewildered look and a map held upside-down and, if the town is West Kirby, you may be rescued by a Ranger from the Wirral Country Park. A native of the town, child chorister and grammar school boy, Chris Bower is full of local lore, and has provided much of this information.

West Kirby, perhaps the Wirral's most ancient settlement, is reached by travelling along the A540 almost the length of this oddly wedge-shaped

Along the Prom.   *John Cocks*

peninsular. By car this affords a breezy approach to a town which nestles where Dee and sea converge and Hilbre Island forms a blob offshore. A pleasanter approach on foot starts from the Wirral Way car park below Caldy village.

How much the Wirral residents owe to Laurence Beswick! His vision led to the creation of this linear park after the closure, in 1962, of the twelve-mile railway connecting Hooton with West Kirby. Thanks to him we now enjoy windswept embankments with views over the Dee to Wales, mysterious cuttings arched by dripping trees, and platform picnic-sites. Glimpses of history too remain; in 1884 the landlord of Caldy's now-defunct Hop Inn made his fortune by rolling barrels of beer on pay-day down to the sweating navvies.

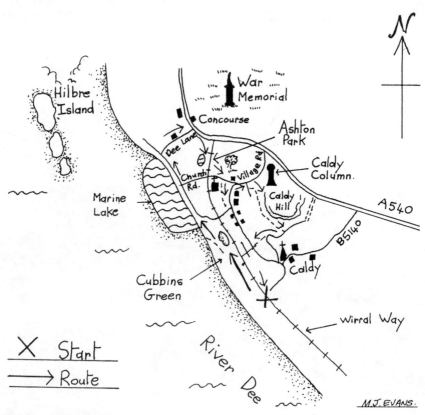

M.J. EVANS.

West Kirby

John Cocks

Pass through the primrose-fringed picnic area to the sheltered path, which, through the slender branches of willow and alder, affords spasmodic glimpses of the shimmering Dee. Look out for hedge laying (the first this century), the sycamore stake tops neatly bound with willow etherings. At an opening to the shoreline (known locally as Cubbins Green) turn left, listening for the sound of both sea and sea birds (their number most prolific in the winter months) and, towards Hilbre Island, both oyster catchers and cocklers may be hard at work.

55

Take the right-hand path, sheltered by coppiced willow, and watch for a white-collared blackbird (descendant of a rare albino) before reaching a pond, recently hollowed to replace clay pits now obliterated by bungalows. Water-loving animals and plants now thrive again -bullrushes, water lilies, yellow flag iris, kingcups and Canadian pond weed - under the stippled shade of whitebeam and oak, with a jack snipe a welcome winter guest.

At low tide you can continue along the beach to the sailing club (otherwise detour via Macdona Drive and Sandy Lane). Then stride the length of the Marine Lake - an ideal base for water sports, its width now doubled in size thanks to an influx of EEC money. At the far end turn right along Dee Lane to the commercial centre of the modern town. Dominated by the drab, grey, Concourse buildings, the area nevertheless bustles with activity.

The Marine Lake, ideal for water sports   *John Cocks*

Opposite is the start of the Wirral Way, its natural borders contrasting with Ashton Park's more formal design, where ducks noisily squabble for titbits on the lake, groaning backs bend over bowling greens, children shout from swing and slide and, in early June the tennis club hosts one of the most prestigious tournaments in England, where famous players perfect their serve and slice, volley and lob, prior to Wimbledon itself.

Leave the Way at the first bridge, turning left up Church Road to the oldest part of the town. The name 'Kirby' is derived from a Norse word meaning church-town, and the early settlers here were composed mainly of Norsemen from Man and Ireland. Continue through the churchyard to St. Bridget's Church - itself named after an Irish saint. Etched indistinctly on the tower's south wall are the remains of a scratch sundial, and a well-seasoned oaken door hides in the church's wall.

Inside, this venerated church boasts an almost unique east window; its burnished glass set into the most delicate stone tracery was designed by C E Kempe - a distinguished Victorian glassmaker. Adjacent to the church, and once a school, the Charles Dawson Brown Museum houses an ancient hogsback tombstone of a pattern prevalent in Viking days.

From here turn left, then left again up Village Road, where cottages of mellowed brick or half-timbered Tudor style front hidden courtyards, and both Moby Dick and Ring o'Bells vie for passing trade. As you climb the slope, the walls of Manor Farm rise out of solid bedrock before you turn right into Wetstone Lane. Then turn immediately left onto Caldy Hill, a heather-clad, sandstone ridge sheltering the town from bitter easterlies. As you gain height views stretch down the North Wales coastline from the Point of Air lighthouse to the Llandudno Ormes. Nearby, the globe-topped Caldy Column was erected in 1841 by the Trustees of Liverpool's docks. A warning beacon for mariners, it replaced the windmill destroyed by a gale two years earlier, and was fashioned from its stone.

Continue past the booster transmitter and the waterworks, where a well sunk 600 feet into triassic sandstone ensures a permanent water supply. The viewfinder was erected here in 1933 - a memorial to local benefactors who saved these slopes from a builder's decimation. Northerly views include the nearest Lakeland mountain of Black Coombe, Winter Hill on the Pennines and, across the Mersey, Liverpool's disparate cathedrals. On the Wirral itself, the chimney pots of Hill Bark peep out from Royden Park; half timbered and mock Tudor it was reassembled here from Bidston Hill - its loss was Royden's gain.

On Grange Hill's adjacent slopes soars the tapering obelisk of the town's war memorial with, around its base, bronze figures embellishing the immortal words of Kipling: *Who stands if freedom fall? Who dies if England live?* Below it, Caldy Grange Grammar School for Boys was

West Kirby's Parish Church is dedicated to the Irish Saint, St. Bridget *John Cocks*

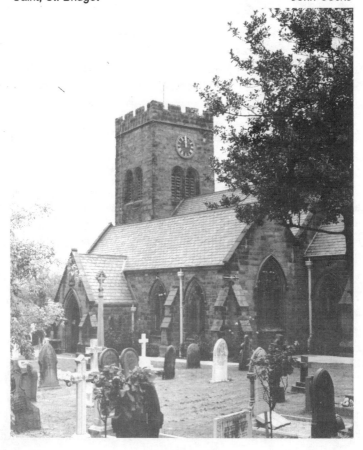

Olde Worlde Cottages at West Kirby   *John Cocks*

founded in 1636 by William Glegg, *'for the good and christian institution of boys ... to instruct them in virtues and good letters for all future time.'* I wonder what he would think of GCSE?

From here continue south along the top path through golden gorse which, when pruned, forms brushwood for the jumps on Haydock racecourse. Look out for sparrow hawks spread-eagled in their flight, lizards basking deathlike on flat stones, or snakes slithering slowly o'er the path. On your left the ancient bridleway of Fleck Lane traverses the hill to Caldy before you reach woodland and veer right then left to open heath, passing invasive rhododendron clumps to rejoin the main path and turn left again.

Walk through a windswept coppice of primeval pines before turning right at a rocky outcrop, its sheer cliffs hiding a plaque and seat where the weary can *'Rest and Be Thankful'*. The path then descends to Kings Drive where you turn right, then right again at the hairpin to re-enter Caldy Hill. From here keep left through a wall-gap, then downhill to Caldy Road, carefully crossing it before plunging down Meloncroft Drive to a final left turn along the Wirral Way.

A lucky day indeed now that walkers can enter West Kirby along this disused track, for what better entrance to the town's marine parade, and then a return route through the older town to the exhilarating slopes of Caldy Hill. And, if the sun is setting as you complete your stroll, mauve and magenta clouds streaking across the sky, you will appreciate how the artist, Turner, found the sunsets here remarkable enough to paint.

Sunset over West Kirby - beloved by Turner *John Cocks*

WHITCHURCH - GATEWAY TO CHESHIRE

Distance: **1 mile**

W hether this should be referred to as a 'Townies' walk or a family walk is perhaps debatable; certainly it is short, circumnavigates the town and has a delightful finish for children. The small, yet bustling market town of Whitchurch stands on the Shropshire border at Cheshire's southern extremity; its narrow streets, and many-styled buildings tumble down from a hilltop church dedicated to St Alkmund.

Entering the town from the north you can't fail to miss the grandeur of the former grammar school, only dating from the middle of the last century but

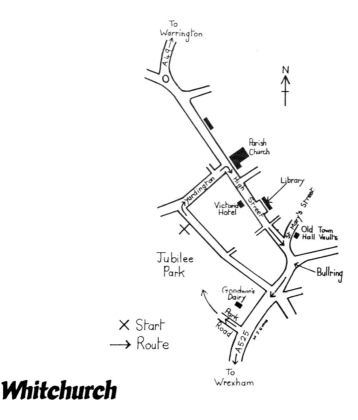

Whitchurch

Whitchurch's lofty church tower bears the handiwork of clockmaker
J. B. Joyce   *John Cocks*

built with a glorious Elizabethan flourish. Tucked away beside it is an older,
brick building with quoins and gables - once a tiny infant school. Then turn
right down Yardington, where a free carpark is on the left.

As you walk back towards the church, a mellow, sandstone wall
commemorates Whitchurch's Roman origin, as also does Roman Way - its

modern memorial. The town's Roman name was, appropriately enough, Mediolanum - the 'town in the middle of the plain' - and several Roman finds have been discovered on the site here, including a unique Roman mirror.

Approaching from this direction affords the best head-on view of the 18th century church - second in size to Shrewsbury itself. Fashioned from rough, red sandstone, its stark, rectangular faces dominate the town; the lofty, balustraded west tower houses a melodic ring of eight bells, while the spacious, airy interior is graced by tall, Tuscan columns and girdled by a wooden gallery.

15th Century building work   *John Cocks*

Opposite is the High Street garage, its undulating roof, bulging walls and 'magpie' frontage all indicative of great age and, dating back to 1450, it may well be the town's oldest building. Continue down the hill to the Victoria Hotel. In the 17th century, when known as the Red Lion (the most common pub name in England), it was a busy coaching inn on the main Chester-Birmingham route when the cock-pit behind provided gruesome and bloody entertainment for both locals and passengers. Serving Burtonwood Real Ale nowadays, it is one of many Whitchurch pubs which provide competitively-priced bar meals.

Housed in a modern building set back from the road, the excellent library, with its helpful staff, is named after Randolph Caldicott, a Victorian illustrator of children's books. Although he only worked in the town as a bank clerk for a few years, some of his later illustrations feature unmistakable Whitchurch scenes, and his character sketches are now featured on the tourist information promoting the town.

The building opposite, decorated by a unique, ironwork facade, once housed the firm of J.B. Joyce - a long-established, local firm of clockmakers. Particularly well-known for the manufacture of station clocks, it is perhaps appropriate that the business is now based in Station Road. Above and behind, the blue and gold turret clock gleams down from the church tower, its brightly-gilded face renewed in 1977 to mark the Queen's Silver Jubilee. The shapely hands are Joyce's hallmark, while the accurate mechanism gives ample evidence of the firm's superb craftsmanship.

Overshadowed by the NatWest Bank - an impressively flamboyant fake only dating from the 1930s - is Ye Olde Coffee Shoppe, suitably trading in premises which partly date from the 15th century, and where once a cooper fashioned barrels and casks, buckets and bowls.

Then turn aside into St. Mary's Street, where the Old Town Hall Vaults are worth a visit for their memorabilia to Sir Edward German, and a marble wall plaque commemorates the composer's birth here in 1862, when it was the Cornmarket Inn. From a musical family, he was brought up in the town, learning to play the organ in the parish church. Also accomplished in piano and violin he studied, then lectured, at the Royal Academy in London. Knighted in 1928, today he is perhaps best remembered for his musical scores for the operettas - 'Merrie England' and 'Tom Jones'.

At the bottom end of the street an assortment of styles and ages mingle together: imposing Tuscan columns front the Midland Bank, while tucked away in a quiet corner is the 15th century White Bear. The Bullring itself, now awash with traffic, was the place where, until 1802, bulls were tethered to a ring in the middle of the road, to be cruelly baited by dogs.

Town Parks & Playgrounds for the younger set   *John Cocks*

Bear right, then right again along the Wrexham Road, where the last pub in England may be plain, and the exhaust fumes unpleasant, but where ivy-covered, terraced cottages lighten the way, their neatly-tended gardens aglow with blooms.

Keep right past the thriving concern of Goodwin's Dairy and Cheesery. Recently extended, its chimney almost vies with the church tower as a local landmark. Both Whitchurch itself, and the surrounding agricultural

65

community, have always been renowned for cheese production, for many years farmers selling their dairy produce in the cheese market behind the Civic Centre. Nowadays, three kinds of Cheshire cheese are still available - the crumbly white, its red-dyed counterpart, and the connoisseurs' soft blue (a deserved rival of Stilton).

A right turn takes you into the quiet terrace of Park Road, with the entrance to Jubilee Park ahead. The breezy football pitch tops a plateau while, in a more sheltered dell, a variety of bushes, trees, and flower borders surround the colourful adventure playground, which boasts no fewer than twelve pieces of apparatus. Opened in 1977 to mark the Queen's Silver Jubilee its tunnel and slide, rope ladder and swings, provide a multitude of opportunities for both child contortionist or more imaginative youngster.

Overlooking the playground, where steep steps lead back to the car park, are the Harry Richards' Memorial Gardens. Named after the owner of a local coach firm, who bequeathed money in his will for the town's benefit, a variety of rose beds surround a neat and compact bandstand. And from the garden's seats one can glimpse the surrounding countryside, where gentle slopes are intersected by slow-moving canals, leisurely country lanes and charming villages.

Whitchurch itself is often referred to as the Gateway to the Potteries, Chester and Wales, and has always been known as a centre for cheese-making; lesser known perhaps, but an integral part of the town, are an impressive church, industrious clock-maker, and illustrious composer.